There's More To It Than That

ALSO BY JEFF WEDDLE

Good Party (Poetic Justice Books, 2020)

Dead Man's Hand (Poetic Justice Books, 2019)

A Puncher's Chance (Rust Belt Press, 2019)

Citizen Relent (Unlikely Books, 2019)

It's Colder than Hell / Starving Elves Eat Reindeer Meat / Santa Claus is Dead (Alien Buddha Press, 2018)

Heart of the Broken World (Nixes Mate Books, 2017)

Comes to This (Nixes Mate Books, 2017)

When Giraffes Flew (Southern Yellow Pine, 2015)

The Librarian's Guide to Negotiation: Winning Strategies for the Digital Age (co-author, Information Today 2012)

Betray the Invisible (OEOCO, 2012)

Bohemian New Orleans: The Story of the Outsider and Loujon Press (University Press of Mississippi, 2007)

There's More To It Than That

poems by
Jeff Weddle

Poetic Justice Books
Port St. Lucie, Florida

©2021 Jeff Weddle

book design and layout: SpiNDec, Port Saint Lucie, FL
cover image: *Mixed Message*, ©2021 Kris Haggblom

All rights reserved.

No part of this book may be used or reproduced in any manner whatsoever without written permission except in the case of brief quotations embodied in critical articles and reviews. Members of educational institutions and organizations wishing to photocopy any of the work for classroom use, or authors, artists and publishers who would like to obtain permission for any material in the work, should contact the publisher.

Published by Poetic Justice Books
Port Saint Lucie, Florida
www.poeticjusticebooks.com

ISBN: 978-1-950433-59-9

FIRST EDITION
10 9 8 7 6 5 4 3 2 1

Always for Jill

the poems

Autobiography	3
School Is in Session	4
Things to Believe	6
Zen Mind Gone	8
The Web	10
It Happens	12
Those Times She Is With Me	14
A Gift	16
Missed Connection	17
You'll Think	18
How It Sometimes Goes	19
Cuts	21
What Passes for Prayer	23
Nothing Else	24
This Foolish Thing	25
In the Bones	27
So Many of Us	28
And So It Goes	31
When There Was Music	33
Thank You	34
Morning After Coffee	36
There's More to It Than That	37
If	38
Then Came Night	39
Last Chance	40
That Girl, Right Over There	41
Maybe You Know Her	42
She Was Too Much. Really.	43

Burning	46
Request	48
The Great Writer	49
Always	51
Step Right Up	53
Walk a Mile	55
Life and Death Are Everywhere	56
Mass Transit Sage	59
Special Event	60
Dreams	61
You'll See	62
Trying Not Trying	63
Do This	64
Inventory	65
The Listing of Things	66
When I Was Beautiful	67
The Poet's Carnage	69
Sabers, Gentlemen! Sabers!	70
Two Ton Tony	72
Piano Haiku	74
The People Are Afraid and the Streets Are Empty	75
Far From Me	76
This Is the Situation	77
Plague Year	78
Virus Morning	79
The Thing Left To Do	81
This Moment in Time	82

Visiting Home	83
Not Everyone Lived	84
I Can't Breathe	87
Beacon	89
Reading Is Fundamental	90
Literary Matters	92
Treasure	94
Nobody's Walking on Water and the Herd Needs Thinning	95
Swimming Hole	96
Something in the Air	98
Our Forever Home	99
You Say You Want a Revelation? Well, You Know….	100
Big Sister	102
Tick Tock	104
Your Friend, the Writer	106
Just Relax	108
And You Alone	109
Be Kind	111
Like Flipping a Switch	112
Here's the Thing	114
Look in the Mirror	115
Scream or Fly	116
Where Things Are Poppin' the Philadelphia Way	118
Weird	120
A Stumper	121
Senescence	122

Praise Jesus Real Loud. I Dare You.	124
One Foot Ahead of the Other	126
Here's to You	128
Road Trip	129
To the Great and Glorious Among Us	131
It's All Magic	134
Soirée	136
Good Night	139
The Loop	141
Raw Nerves and Strangers	142
Final Notice	143
Dear Reader	145

There's More To It Than That

Autobiography

I am made
of ink
and dreams

and all
the world
is paper

School Is in Session

There are lessons
to be found
everywhere

like in random notes
played on the keys
on an old piano

the mute grace
observed
in the orbits
of celestial bodies

or the slow stride
of an ancient cat
across a dull
wooden floor.

There are lessons
in harmonics
and discord
and other mysteries.

The old masters
understood this
even as they
disagreed
on their meaning.

Lessons you would
do well
to notice

as you busy yourself
with silly things

like the love
who will never have you

or her touch

or life or death
or tomorrow.

Things to Believe

The first illusion is joy
golden and flesh

hard breath
and auburn hair
across a damp neck.

Then comes rage
illusion second class

hot destroyer
of illusion one.

No damp neck
for you.

And apathy follows.

That's real.
So sorry.

The last illusion
is forgetting

but you
knew that
already.

But here's
the thing:

Everything happens
all at once
forever.

You know?

The sages wonder:

Why do we
even bother
with goodbye?

Zen Mind Gone

Your Zen mind
has taken a powder.

It's off somewhere
in the void
and does not miss you.

Your Zen mind
is the sound
of one hand
giving you the finger
in perfect silence.

It is the fragrance of blue
the rhythm of stone.

Your Zen mind may return
but don't bet the bathtub.

It is the thunderclap
hidden beneath the doormat
so the forgetful universe
can get inside.

It needs nothing but infinity
and you have none to spare.

Your Zen mind is off
being a holy tramp
not even waving
goodbye

but say goodbye anyway
if you like.

Nothing matters to
your Zen mind.

That prick.

The Web

What if Charles Bukowski
had never lived
or beautiful Paula Hinchman?

What if I had never known
my childhood friends
like Randy Burruss
or Marty Osborne or Doonie Ward?

What if I had not drunk vodka
with Mike Fitzpatrick
or started on beer
with John Spears?

Or what about beautiful Vicky Hill
and David Banner and Tom Blackburn
and Philip Bishop?

What if I hadn't gotten into karate
when I was fourteen?

What if beautiful Margaret
had not been at that high school reunion?

Or what if I never read Brautigan
and really what if Bukowski
had never been born?

What if I had never found my Jill
through all of it?

That's the terrifying question.

What if I had not found her?

What then would have become
of me?

It Happens

Sometimes it happens
that you meet a candle

the impossible kind
that lights up a downpour

or burns brightest
in a convertible
top down at 90
on an empty highway
cutting night
to the bone.

Sometimes
but not very often
you meet a witch
who really can fly
and doesn't need potions
to make you love her
but has them ready
just in case.

Sometimes you meet a woman
who will play chess naked
like it's the most natural thing
in the world

and beat you
with her intelligence
even as you try not to stare.

Sometimes you wait
lifetimes
for her to appear

maybe in a white cotton dress
or adorned in rubies and silver

electric as your fetished imaginings
mythic as the young Earth
or outlandish dreams
of flesh.

Those Times She Is With Me

Every night it's one thing or the other.
I buy a 12 pack on the way home from work
and either she shows up to help me drink it
or she doesn't.

If she does, we sit on the love seat
and listen to music
and talk about every crazy thing
you can imagine.

On those nights she doesn't come
I drink my beer and pace.

Those nights can be very bad,
the walls too straight and solid
and time dragging me to the next time,
pulling out small parts of me,
but never enough to do the job.

She'll be 24 in a few days
and she smiles in her sleep.

I have watched her like that for hours,
fascinated by the smallest things:
the breath entering and leaving her body
her hair against the pillow
that small, daisy tattoo
and the way she sleeps like the dead.

But she wakes, leaves me,

and there is nothing left but the walls,
the alarm clock
and morning
so dark and chill and unwanted.

A Gift

beautiful girl
on a skateboard

black mini dress
and frizzy hair

on an August day
in Alabama

here for a second
and gone

trailing dreams
and summer scorch

somehow alone
and shining

this heartbreaker
in cool shades

rolling right on
down the line

Missed Connection

In the turning I missed
seeing the one
who would have loved me
with her long legs
and auburn hair.

I missed seeing her blue eyes
and the funny sweater
she borrowed from her sister
just for that afternoon.

I missed seeing her at all
and that was that.

I never saw her before
or after
so missing her
just then
was quite a loss.

In the turning I made
a different connection
and likely she did too

and I suppose each of us
is content

and whatever her name
and wherever she is

I hope she is in love.

You'll Think

You'll think about it later
maybe even years from now.

You'll think about
the angle of light
in that room
on that particular day

about her sitting
on that green couch
her legs crossed in denim

the weight of the air
the beguiling fragrance
the stolen glances.

You'll think about her hair
falling across her shoulders
and how she laughed
at something you didn't say.

You'll think about
the one you never spoke to
the thing you never said.

How It Sometimes Goes

Take the dancer
for instance
washing her hair

half drunk

with her wet
black hair
and crying.

The lovely dancer
in her lingerie.

Take the dancer
alone in a small room
with her bourbon
and wet hair

beautiful
in black silk.

She would tell you
cheap bourbon
is a poor excuse
for a lover.

She would
tell you this
slurring her words
in silk lingerie

wet black hair
dripping
on the floor.

She would tell you this
as you hold a telephone
in a dark hall
many miles from
that small room

as you stand there
stupid and alone
bleeding regret
and let her dance away.

Cuts

I am wounded
and it has nothing
to do with you

but you get the jagged result

and I do not even know
where the wound
came from

but it has been with me
for as long as I can remember

and sometimes
I can barely breathe

and I often want to cry

and conversation
is beyond possibility

and my guess is you
are also wounded

and it has nothing
to do with me

but you can cut me
if you need to find
someone to cut

I understand

and can brace myself
past the screams
and the dark silence

and those times
we embrace
and forget
will be as healing
as all the years
lost

retrieved by some magic
from these flames
we have so long
endured

What Passes for Prayer

It is nice to lie alone
on a small bed
in a dark room
as the world
somehow
keeps spinning

and consider the possibility
that things will turn out fine.

The odds are bad,
but we are still alive
there is wine to drink
and somewhere
there are lovers
who cannot imagine
they will ever give up.

It is nice to think
of their happiness
right this second

of soft kisses
the surprise of joy
and easy laughter.

It is nicer to believe
in the chance
they are right.

Nothing Else

There are first kisses
and broken bones

lost trinkets
of silver and glass.

Sometimes
there is spice
from an unexpected hand

small books
which carry more
than words

the last snow of winter
and the first

hard winds to make
the waters dance

years which flow
into years

into days
that cannot
be imagined

first kisses
and a final embrace

the nod at the end
of the dance.

This Foolish Thing

The task is impossible.
Words are not enough

nor silence
nor intimate touch
nor art of any sort
nor science
nor reason
nor God.

It cannot be done
through the preparation
or sharing
of an exquisite meal

or any communal tragedy
or a drive
across the continent
in a small car.

Even with decades together
the task cannot
be finished.

You can never know me
not truly
nor I you

and worse
you can never
know yourself.

The person
you might have been
if you had worn a green shirt
on a particular day
instead of blue

or read different books
at different times

or loved this person
instead of that one

but we try
impossibly.

The task
is all we know.

It is what endures.

We tell ourselves
it is enough.

In the Bones

It was that one day
in October
let's say 1978

that one day
when everything worked.

Let's say there was a girl

and of course
there was music

the kind of music
you feel more than hear

but you feel it always
like your fingers
touching her hair.

1978 was like that
especially October
and that one day

when the pieces fit

and all the maps
took us home.

So Many of Us

Some are strangers
in this world

awkward and sullen

uninterested
in the pleasures
upon which the masses
agree.

Saints and psychopaths
nudists
thieves
readers of books
often the insane
or homeless
or young children

maybe strippers
or mail carriers
or grocery clerks
garbage collectors
butchers
poets
and the more interesting
librarians.

You will find them
on barstools
and wandering city streets
or maybe walking alone
in graveyards
near sunset.

You will sometimes find them
in your bed
or sitting across the table
at the evening meal

showing themselves
with an odd glance
or stray gesture
that reveals all
that has been hidden
for decades.

Some people
are strangers
in this world:

the vicious
the mad
the pure at heart.

My people

in search of something
they cannot name
and will never find.

Each one a gift

though gifts
can be bad
and even the best
of them will
often disappoint

and, believe me,
even your dearest
will sometimes bite.

And So It Goes

Naked and forgetting
the safety of sheets
she stands by
a dirty window
of dead flies
and open curtains

gazing at
the half-empty
parking lot.

A young man
walking to his car
fails to notice
her accidental gift
of beauty

his mind caught
on the one
he has abandoned
in a different room

while her puzzled lover
asks again
why she has left the bed

and the young man
starts his car
and pulls away

with no idea
where the night
will take him

and she says aloud
she is not sure
why she was
ever there
at all.

When There Was Music

All the directions
a body might move
hers moved
at once and together
so that the sidewalks
became music
and the trees a ballet.

Hailstorm and lightning
stood no chance
against her rhythm

and in the sheets
she became the serpent

and in the air
she became the clouds.

All the directions
had their own notes
and everyone wanted
her tune

but she danced and danced and danced
into the blaze of gone away

and I went nowhere

in that silent afternoon
of the tone deaf and useless
god damned empty
suddenly empty
god damned
world.

Thank You

This is for
my first love
and my last
and all those
in between

for the ones
who loved me back
and those who never did

for those who wronged me
and the ones
I casually hurt.

This is for long
October walks
and movies shared
in darkness

hot tender nights
and screams

tears and laughter
the long silence
and the hard leaving.

This is for years
spent too fast
and especially
for times
of grace.

This is for each one on the wind
the music we shared
or could have.

This is for love
for you
and nothing ever lost
or forgotten.

Morning After Coffee

Photographs
on the refrigerator

and an empty cup

orange tablecloth
pepper shaker and pills

the house quiet
and everyone sleeping

all the aches of age

keys to an old car
and nowhere to go

There's More to It Than That

"Things are not
so simple," she said
removing the skin
from my face.

"Things are far more
complex," she said
separating my leg
from my hip.

"Things get screwed up
sometimes," she said
pulling my lungs
through my nose.

"Things are truly
fucked," she said
telling me goodnight
without so much
as a kiss.

If

If I found you
laughing
I would laugh
with you.

If I found you
crying
I would cry.

And if found you
dismembering
a body

I would
creep away
slowly
oh so slowly
into the night.

Then Came Night

When everything
was gone
but framed photographs
of relatives
no one remembered

he took his favorite cup
from the cabinet
and drove to the place
they had chosen to meet.

She watched
as the truck got close
then walked to the curb.

He handed her
a small silver thing
that meant nothing
to anyone in the world
and drove away.

No one cried

and when the house burned
in the dying autumn light
you could see the flames
for miles

if you thought to look.

Or, like the two of them,
you could pretend not to notice
and make a point to regret it later.

Last Chance

Kissing her
on a sidewalk
in the rain
old cars
crawling past
as one person
stands watch
behind a dark
window.

"I love you"
someone says
in this moment
that lasts forever
as the rain falls
and eyes meet
and no one
ever knows
how it ends.

That Girl, Right Over There

She tries on attitudes
the way a peacock
tries on hats,

awkwardly
and with great
abandon.

Don't judge.

She might love you
if you let her,

but no promises.

Either way
she becomes
a rainbow

in shades
of true blessing

and, even to save your soul,

you will never guess
her meaning.

Maybe You Know Her

Tall girl with red hair
eyes taking in the mysteries

you might say she's lanky.

Brave girl in the wind
speaking her mind
speaking plain

confident in stride
and magnetic
in stillness.

Tall girl cozy with trees
simply on first names
with daisies
as much as owls and lizards.

Sunshine
seeks her out
like a timid suitor

stunned by her
brilliant soul

fearful
halting

and so much in love.

She Was Too Much. Really.

At the counter she asked for all the magic,
every bit of it.

Everyone knew this was selfish,
beyond selfish, really,
but she was who she was
so the clerk handed it over,
every bit.

All the potions and spells,
the amulets and so forth,
the capes and hats and wands.

Somehow he even gave her
all the nudity.

You should have seen her
dolled up like Merlin
and the Oracle at Delphi
and the guy who did magic shows
at your grade school
for fifty cents a head
and butt naked
all at the same time.

She took all the magic
and went around imposing her will
and even her unconscious desires
in huge bursts of witchery.

All over people fell in love
with themselves
with one another
with her.

Mostly with her.

And every reptile
gained the power of flight
dogs and cats danced the rhumba
as they discoursed on Proust
all that.

It was crazy

but when you have all the magic
that's what you do.

Now get away from me.

You never know
when she'll walk through a wall
or slither beneath a door
or if she's standing here now
invisible
taking us in.

I don't want to be turned inside out
or made to give anal pleasure
to a crew of mythical beings

because she has mommy and daddy issues
or indigestion
or she's just feeling kinky.

Leave me alone. I mean it.

No one no one no one
wants to be noticed.

And none but the mad
can stand it
when she becomes
the face of the moon
licks her almighty lips
and smiles benevolently
upon even the most wretched
of we mortal creatures here below.

Burning

When she lost hope
she became brave

and, being brave,
she found strength

and strong,
she became a beacon

and the people saw this
and they became fire for her

and their fire
became the world

and their fire
became the way

and their fire
became her glory

when all that remained
was memory

and the hope of brave things
like a blood garland

across time
everyone caught

and tearful
believing it all

in the crumbling hours
of the crumbling world

Request

You, traveler, must be strong.

You must be the dying runner
who will not quit the race,
the broken fighter
who swings from the floor,
the fool who loves in vain.

You are the light, the last chance,
the straw we all hope to grasp.

Be the music that taught you glory.

Take it on.
Fight for the world.

Victory may be impossible,
but there is no other option.

The Great Writer

Of course, no one noticed.
Why would they?

He was nobody,
and his art was out of step with the times.

And besides, it was so incredibly vulgar
that even his wife wouldn't read it

though he dedicated it,
like everything he did, to her.

So, he papered his walls
with pages ripped

from the many copies of the book
he had purchased from the publisher,

and he sprayed these pages with lighter fluid,
and touched a match to one thin edge.

And his wife, who sat with him in that room,
would have screamed,
had her mouth not been taped shut.

And she would have fought,
had her arms not been bound.

And she would have run,
had her feet not been broken.

And so they watched, these two,
as his words glowed with fire,

as he had always believed they would.

And, for a day or two after that, he was known,
if still woefully misunderstood.

Always

You walk through the door and hear the crashing.
It's odd, because before you opened the door
everything was quiet.

Now, it's so loud you can't think.

You walk through the door
and the lights hurt your eyes.
So many colors, each one new and brighter
than colors have a right to be,
colors you wish you could describe,
but words don't exist for any of them.

You walk through the door
and hear the crashing and see the people.
You see the people running like crazy.
You see the people dancing.
You see the people fighting
and yelling unintelligible words.
You see the people making love and firing weapons.

Sheila finds you.
She takes your arm and leads you to the edge.
Past the edge there is nothing.
No lights, no crashing, no people.
Sheila leads you past the edge.
She is hungry and takes your flesh as her meal.
She shreds you and eats every bite.

You are now entirely Sheila
and she is entirely you.
You emerge into a desert.
It is finally night and the stars sing.
You are in love.

What could be worse?

You forget who you were before you became Sheila.
Then you forget Sheila.

You fall into the place before.
You fall into the crashing.
You become the nameless colors.

There is a door somewhere
and beyond that door is the whole world.
You move with the rhythm of weapons firing.
You move with the logic of color.

Everything is dance.

You are the nameless time.
Finally, you understand flow
and everything happens.

Everything happens.
Everything happens.

Step Right Up

Hindenburg
Titanic
Jack the Ripper
Ebola AIDS
cancer COVID-19 ALS
straight razor in the bathtub
razor blades in apples
poison candy poison intent poison mind
bullet to the head bullet to the back
bullet to the neck bullet to the heart
bullet with your name on it
bad air bad food bad water
cigars cigarettes Tiparillos
hidden burns shameful cuts
decades in a bad job
bad marriage
World Trade Center Pentagon
police officers with their hate
dead liver dead prostate dead lungs
no home but inside the skull
no home but the tiny room
no home but the street
no home but regret
heart attack diabetes stroke
degenerative disease all kinds
bone rot brain rot life rot
the Beverly Hills Supper Club fire
fires in movie theaters

trailer park tornadoes
mass shootings wherever you like
strangers who follow you home
clowns who eat little boys
little boys who eat acquaintances
women who can no longer cope
the school bus in the river
gas leaks stalkers surveillance
wrong turn at the wrong time
failure to turn failure to notice
failure to care failure to try
Hindenburg
Titanic
Jack the Ripper
pick your ticket
choose your ride

Walk a Mile

Put yourself in the fly's shoes.

It doesn't understand your broken swatter.
It has no concept of your hate.

It only knows something huge
and terrible
is after it.

It only knows
it wants to rest in the sun.

It just wants to eat garbage
and be left alone.

Put yourself in the fly's shoes.
It shouldn't be too hard.

Huge and terrible things
are everywhere.

Enjoy the sun
and your evening meal.

Be ready, if you are able,
for what is to come.

Be ready for the catastrophe
you will never understand.

Life and Death Are Everywhere

Gin drunk boy
stumbles along
the winter sidewalk
counting angels
in his head
sometimes
forced to rely
on fingers and toes
because angels
multiply fast
die faster
and are often
too tricky
for anybody's
good.

The old lady
riding the Number 9 bus
removes a
halo from her purse
and tosses it
out the window
as the bus passes by
striking the gin drunk boy
on the head
to the delight
of her fellow
passengers

while she smiles
and moves closer
to her funeral
only a week away.

She does not care
that in the whole world
there is no one
who will remember
any of this
longer than
the life
of a mayfly.

The angels
remain far away
and unaware
of the old lady
the boy
or the bus

and go about
their killing
of innocent dreams
as though nothing
in heaven or earth
could ever matter.

The old lady
exits the bus
at her regular stop
takes three flights of stairs
to her small apartment
where the memory
of an old cat
claws her heart

and dreams
of all the sins and comfort
to be found
in a hot and loving
cup of tea.

Mass Transit Sage

The old man
on the bus
scratched his cheek
and said to no one
in particular,
"I miss everyone
I ever
loved
and myself
most of all."

The bus filled with silence
like the roots of trees
as he stood
and exited into
history.

I'll be damned
if I've had
a good night's sleep
since.

Special Event

What is this cadaver
splayed on the kitchen table?

This rotting thing
with the face of an angel
and wings still capable of flight?

What are these things
still alive inside?

How is it that they dance?

Only loud prayers are heard,
if you really want to know.

Scream them out.
Get this thing into the air.

Sing with me the lost songs.
Bring love to the hollows of time,
if you are able.

You must understand
and explain to the others:

We are out of options
and there are no places
left to hide.

Dreams

I sometimes dream
that I am living

that this body
does not rot
inside the earth.

I sometimes dream
I am alive

and then I wake
and know the truth.

I sometimes dream
I am you
with all
that comes with
your life.

These are all
the very worst things

these shadows

these dreams
which will not
let me be.

You'll See

The dead grow with time
great piles of memory
and strips of our own flesh
reaching toward the heat
of an imagined star

blooming fast
into puppet theater

Punch and Judy playing dress up
for an audience of one.

Bodies gone to earth
so many bodies
empty in the grave
become bit players and leads
in our dwindling new stories
and no one is surprised
when they fade to exit
without so much
as a curtain call
or when the years
no longer matter.

Trying Not Trying

I could do nothing if I tried.
I'm certain of it.

Nothing at all.

I can already sit and stare.
That's almost doing nothing.

I'm sure, if I put my mind to it,
I could do much less.

Less than you, anyway.

I mean, for God's sake,
you're reading this.

What are you,
a hive of ambition?

I can do nothing at all,
believe me.

Nada.

I can do it for hours
just as a warm up
to something even less.

Watch me.

Or don't.

Here goes....

Do This

Believe what your spirit knows
and go forth with courage.

All that can be *is*, of course,
though the game changes
moment by moment.

You laughed when I said
we are wild roots dreaming
in an echo of time
but, in your secret heart,
you always knew.

I tell you plainly
that we have loved forever
and nothing has been lost.
Go forth and be.

Return as you will.
This is my only command.

Inventory

Robert Anton Wilson
and Edna St. Vincent Millay
Sylvia Plath
the Lone Ranger
Cowboy Bob
blood pooling on a dirty sidewalk
broken streets
broken strangers
the girls you loved and lost
the one you loved more
but never had
trees clear cut
poison air
water unfit for animals
Ernest Hemingway
and Rodney Dangerfield
bad jokes told at your funeral
or just at your expense
Charles Bukowski
and Raymond Carver
the girls you loved in school
age and cuts so deep
they can't be real
your empty heart
the weight of being human
the murder of days
the poetry of the desolate
the damned
the worthy
and me

The Listing of Things

The progression of hours
and a certain quality of light
through half-closed blinds.

A framed print
of a famous painting
tilting between windows.

All strength fading.

Who are you now
old man
sunk into a red couch
stuck here
with no idea of the time?

When I Was Beautiful

When I was beautiful
and the words flowed
I understood things
I cannot now name:

the secrets locked
in trees felled by time

the sounds of an empty day
how babies fly

and all the ways
the dead dream.

When I was electric
the world opened its arms
and many times kissed my hair
and rubbed soft fingers
over my closed eyes.

When I was yours
the sky would never fall
and forever was not enough
let alone possible.

When I was beautiful
I knew both how to strut
and when.

When I faded out no one noticed.

There were so many still dancing
so many who were beautiful
for a while.

When I was beautiful
the ugly world
raced hard
to consume me
and it did.

I never saw it coming.

The Poet's Carnage

At the typewriter
in a white cotton undershirt
and torn boxers

the struggle to create
like a fist fight
between milquetoast poseurs
stuttering curses
on a broken hayride

sometimes Bach on the radio

water glass half empty of bourbon
ashtray overflowing with butts
blood smeared postcards
bearing cryptic messages
mailed from a dozen
small Midwestern towns
each one tacked
to a map of the US

an old Bowie knife
and visions of starving Jesus

somewhere a dog barks

somewhere out there
is the one
attempting contact

somewhere in a corn field most likely
somewhere under a harvest moon

Sabers, Gentlemen! Sabers!

Barry Hannah went mad in Tuscaloosa
and wrote immortal books
drunk as hell and dying of love.

Somewhere there's a little green house
where he wrote *Ray*
and every once in a while stepped into the yard
hoping his ex-wife might drive by so he could wave.

Tuscaloosa is where he shot holes
in the floorboard of his convertible
to let the rain out
because who has time
to put up the top in bad weather
when the words and the booze
won't let you be?

Barry Hannah went mad in Tuscaloosa,
where he lived in a mansion
before his wife wised up and kicked him out.

He went mad in Tuscaloosa
and didn't pay his taxes
and went to jail
and to the lunatic asylum.

Barry Hannah went mad in Tuscaloosa
and is even dead
and I can still hear his footsteps.

Tuscaloosa didn't deserve him
and I never hear a soul mention his name.

Now he's flying high
the battles fought to a bloody nub
and them Yankees running
like Robert E. Lee is nibbling on their bellies.

He was my kind and I have followed
thinking of Barry Hannah
and going mad in Tuscaloosa.

Two Ton Tony

Those days of Two Ton Tony Galento
and circus clowns
midgets with eye patches
and hand-rolled cigarettes.

Good whiskey.

The late night rendezvous
with women of low character
and no expectations.

Two Ton Tony was short and fat
and had no skills
but his left hook
was murder.

Just ask Joe Louis.

He had his bar
all the beer in the world
and everyone cheering.

Forget that he wrestled an octopus
and fought a kangaroo
and a bear.

And that he wouldn't bathe
for days before a fight

and stank like rotten tuna
and bad liquor
just to get an advantage
in the ring.

Galento never ducked anybody
and one time knocked out
three bums
in one night.

Nobody else ever did that
not even until now.

Two Ton Tony, the pride
of Orange, New Jersey.

He could have been champ
but he never was

though he sure
was somebody.

Piano Haiku

I wrote a piano haiku
which no one understands.

You try getting a perfect instant
into seventeen notes
and breaking somebody's heart
with a bird on the wing
in middle C.

You'll know then.

It's like finding love on a bus in Prague
when you were certain you were alone
on a bicycle heading toward Cleveland.

These things are never simple
and it's all a mystery

but everything becomes a poem
if you let it.

The People Are Afraid and the Streets Are Empty

the sickness is everywhere
and people are dying

the people watch
their televisions
and search for hope
but there is no hope to find

the people are afraid
and famous people are dying

and old people and children
are very sick and dying

and the hospitals don't have enough beds
as doctors and nurses are dying

and many years from now
our children's children's children
will wear bright clothing
and laugh
and one day hear our stories
in their schools

and will not even wonder
about us at all

as they drift through
their miracle days
bored that we
were even here

that they need to be told
the dead stories of our time

Far From Me

I teach my class and let them go early
so I can watch TV with my daughter
and we huddle together in bed
wrapped in blankets
pulled into *Stranger Things*

and for some reason I look at my phone
and there it is
John Prine
dead from the virus

and I remember the first time
I heard his songs
and the last time

and the world becomes brittle
as people die everywhere
and my daughter asks me
what's wrong

and there is nothing I can tell her
I can't even speak
as she asks again
and the music stops for now

This Is the Situation

To me be the glory
and the wreckage
I have gathered:

hearts broken
in late August

small pieces
of silver attached
to cold skin

and ice blue eyes
which see
the hard stones
not yet placed
in our way.

Memories of
the last good time
make the leaving
harder

when rescue
is the last resort

but unlikely

given all that sticks
to the plague

we have become.

Plague Year

The streets are
too empty
for tears
and the air is clean
while the people
hide away
and the birds
dance their dances
and we all
wait around
for death
or something
better
though the way
things are going
who's to say
what that
something
might
even be?

Virus Morning

And now I'm crying
over an old song
in the quiet morning
with my dog beside me
on the couch

and the people locked away

and I can't stop the tears
as the song
tells me stories
of before.

In the kitchen
I will eat my breakfast
and tell myself
I will find a way
to stop all this crying
before my children
wander into the room
and ask why daddy is sad

because I don't want
to say the truth
or lie to them.

I just need to keep them safe

though I don't know
how to do that

as the world spins foul
and the people
are hidden
sick and dying

and the music plays.

The Thing Left To Do

Everyone come
we must bury our dead.

The fields are heavy
and we must bury what is left
of our dead
stinking in the bright sun.

The past is impossible
and we must hurry now
and bury our dead.

Everyone come
with the tools you can muster.

Come to the agreed upon place
and bury our dead.

Everyone silent
as we dig our graves
mute in the blistering sun
all questions answered
as we dig our graves.

Our music gone empty
and everyone alone
digging our graves.

Our throats too dry to swallow
as we bury our dead

our silent dead
beckoning in the beautiful sun.

This Moment in Time

What matters now
is the heart

life

the relentless push
of basic muscle.

What matters now
is laughter

and memories of touch.

All the faces we have been –
what of them?

What is hidden remains safe, some of it.

We are unmasked.

I am fragile.
We are the same.

What matters now
is who we find ourselves to be
in how we show love.

Like always, what matters
is who we might
finally become.

Visiting Home

On the church steps
with grey and purple clouds
and the night songs
of animals
cars going somewhere
with their lights and noise
fireflies and a man running
as my father
back at the house
is caught
in a failing body
barely able to move
in his ancient black recliner
and my mother watches him
for signs of need
but seeing none
settles on
cleaning his denture
in this last
bit of smoke
when we are all
still alive
trying to understand
each mystery
except
how lonely
the end can be

Not Everyone Lived

Phil sure didn't.
He kept rage inside
and around him
like an aura
of false smiles
and forced laughter
and drank
until his pancreas
told him to go
fuck himself.

Danny drank
until he turned yellow
then orange
then dead.

David was crazy
first of all
and then there was
all that vodka
for all those years
until his liver
told him to get bent.

with Tom it was pills
and liquor
and god knows what
and then the liver
flipped him off
while he was hoping
for a transplant.

Eric smoked and drank
without ceasing
and didn't give a fuck
about anything
and finally
the cancer came.

Doonie made it home
from Iraq
with so much
poison in him
it was just
a matter of time
though that time
stretched decades.

Donna got cancer
for no good reason.

The nice lady
at the vet's office
was just gone
one day.
I think it was
her heart.

And these are
only the ones
I knew well
or truly liked
or counted
as friends.

So many
gone
from disease
and drinking
drugs
suicide
murder.

And here I sit

old and fat
bad knees
bad shoulders
bad back
bad mind
bad attitude
bad intentions

more or less fine

as the world
becomes still
and small

missing a few
of the vanished

and waiting
for whatever
is to come.

I Can't Breathe

This is how
we burn
city by city
and all
at once

the people
fed up

the people
standing straight
at last

the people
saying
stop killing us

admit it
America
you crazy bitch
you lunatic baby
you spoiled psychopath
raging
for death

your knee
on the people's
neck

this is how
we explode
this is how
we can never
go back

this is how we burn
and burn
and burn

Beacon

What can we say
about the one window
glowing in the night?

The one house
with one window
glowing?

The light escaping
toward the silence
of empty streets?

What can we know
about the reason
behind the light?

There was a hand
which flipped a switch.
There was a soul.

Accident or intent?

Some are drawn
to the light
and some
fear it.

Where will we be
when it is gone?

Reading Is Fundamental

When we discovered
the lost novel
we were afraid
to read it.

Perhaps, some said,
the words
were poison
or would lead
to madness.

Maybe it would be
offensive
to the hysterical professors
who work so hard
to save us
from ourselves.

When we discovered
the lost novel
we did not see its wings.

Many were amazed
when it leapt
from its hiding place
and flew into the sun

lost this time forever
unread
and mocked
all its glories
murdered

leaving us to our smug fears
and so very pleased
in our savage mediocrity.

Literary Matters

In some small book
on a shelf

in a house no one
visits

in some small book
no one will ever read

there is a poem
written about you.

In a town where people
have given up

there is a poem
in a small book

and that poem
tells your fate

a brief poem
of haphazard music

in a house on a street
no one ever knew

but it is there
waiting

this poem written
only for you.

It is there
this poem on the shelf

in the house
waiting forever

decorating your dreams
and adorning the desperate pages.

Treasure

Destiny hidden
in old books
silent poems
unread for decades
souls akimbo in time
fingertips away
from knowing
their blood kindred.

Words that shock
you awake
in hot tears
and laughter.

There is no luck
more precious
than finding what
you truly need
in what you did not
know was lost.

Nobody's Walking on Water and the Herd Needs Thinning

We have had enough of your cross and blood.
Have you had enough of ours?

Can we now burn your temples?
Can we chase away the preachers
who would see the Earth burn in your name?

The money changers were only the future.

There was always a light of the world
but no one saw it true. Now look at us.

There was always a light but you eclipsed it
and now your people bathe in our blood.

And now your people
are fat and stupid
with their whips.

Nothing changes.

The Romans had it right.
Bring on the lions.

Swimming Hole

There may be snakes
in the water

probably there are snakes

and sharp rocks
in the shallows

there are also leeches

you can be certain
there are leeches

and all manner
of slick, biting things

but the water is cool
and it is such a heavy day

there may be disease
in the dark water
and sudden pits
for drowning

there may be ghosts
of missing children
and bodies
still tangled in vines

there may be broken glass
and poison

but it is so hot
and the water feels
delicious

it is best to jump head first
someone said

it is best to get your head under
right away

it is best
not to think about it

it is best to love
the things impatient
to devour you

Something in the Air

1950s radio
broadcasts
filled with lingerie
and perfume
dance inside
the old people
you see
on busses
or laboring
along the sidewalk
propped against
cheap canes
their hands
clutching coins
made of promises
given on lost
summer nights
that seem
barely
an hour gone

Our Forever Home

I wish I could say
I did not choose
this tree
from which I hang

any more than you
chose your own tree

but of course that's wrong.

We looked close
at all the finest trees
elbowing each other
for the best spots
and here we are

swinging in the wind

with our black tongues out
and flies swarming everywhere

dressed at last
in our finest silk
our souls and eyes eaten
by the ravenous
and loving birds.

You Say You Want a Revelation? Well, You Know....

God comes up to me on the street.
Says, "Hey, pally-pally, how's tricks?"

"Tricks is good," says I.

God stares off down the street
where rats are eating the corpse
of an old woman
who died walking home
from her crummy waitress job.

"This shit makes me want to puke," says God.
"What a fucking mess."

"I don't mind," says I.
"But if YOU don't like things,
why not fix it all?"

"I didn't say I didn't like it.
I just said it makes me want to puke," says God.

"Damn, bro," says I.
"You sure work in mysterious ways."

"You know it," says God,
giving me a fist bump. "Stay chill."

"Chillin'," says I.

God walks down the street
and picks the biggest rat
off the old woman's body
and shoves it in his mouth.

Swallows it whole.

"Mysterious ways," he yells back at me.
And then the whole world ends, just like that.

Big Sister

God's sister, Sally, didn't have any awesome powers
and wasn't especially holy
but she was tough and could be kind when she wanted,
or kind of a bitch, depending on her mood.

Being the older child, she took it as her right
to push God around
and call him a twerp, steal his lunch money,
all the stuff that big sisters still like to do
down here among the people.

When God created the universe, Sally rolled her eyes
and patted him on the head.

Told him it was nice work, then gave him a purple nurple
before getting ready for her date with Kronos,
a real bad boy that God called a loser
but secretly admired
with more than a touch of jealousy.

Sally didn't give two fucks what God thought about anything,
but he was, after all, family.

She felt so bad about the nurple thing
that she couldn't really enjoy her date,
even with all the mighty fornication.

When she got home she woke God
and told him every hot detail,
which naturally got him all flustered.

Then they sat together while time began and ended
a thousand thousand times,
finally knowing all there was or ever would be
and said their goodbyes.

As everyone knows, they were never seen again.

Tick Tock

The beating of the heart
the blood in its flow

the body
in its passage through time

children's tears
kites in just-so wind
the needs never met

oatmeal on a quiet morning

an old dog refusing food
the mind unraveling

itchy skin and wrinkles
books no one will read

good hot coffee

an old cat demanding love

closed doors
regret
nerves gone haywire

each day a glittering gift
wrapped in heavy hours

like an old friend
forgetting your face
or stones crashing
down a mountain

pushing us
ever faster

toward the dirt

Your Friend, the Writer

Your friend, the writer, needs groceries:
kale wine ground beef potatoes beer bread
bourbon spaghetti & sauce gin rum ham
mayo absinthe milk Snickers fish sticks
vodka scotch rye ayahuasca peyote
weed and Spam.

Your friend, the writer, needs readers
love hate notice explication a good woman
a bad woman a dog a cat a publisher
an editor and a bookie with a heart.

Your friend, the writer, needs a priest
a rabbi a hooker a nun a Smith and Wesson six shooter
fifty boxes of shells a dozen Spanish orphans
a plot of land and a shovel.

Your friend, the writer, needs earthworms
pickles shears rope caviar statues of Napoleon
pens poison cigarettes laughter and bombs.

Your friend, the writer, needs your wife
your daughter your blood skin bone flesh
muscle soul a quick nap a good night's sleep
a beating heaven and hell.

Your friend, the writer, sends his regards
confusion congratulations regrets condolences
phobias love ambivalence spleen and contagion.

Your friend, the writer, wanders in
wanders out stares at the ceiling
bites his fingernails scratches his ass
smells his fingers yawns and giggles
stares at the mailbox
tries to remember your name
and doesn't write anything at all.

Just Relax

Nothing real is named
nor do we find it with our eyes.

Our hands cannot hold real things
and they have no taste
no sound.

Nothing real will comfort you.
Nothing real dances on the wind
or purrs beside you on your couch
demanding love with sharp claws

as the world pummels everyone
and the charade spins on forever
and we blink on and off

like Christmas lights
on a plastic tree

rescued for a while
from a dark, unknowable
attic.

And You Alone

Who shall let this world
be beautiful?

In spite of the cheats

in spite of the blood-choked air

who shall let this world
be beautiful?

Who shall survive
the hate
and endure?

Who shall understand
this last chance
and seek it?

Who shall forgive?

Who shall offer everything?

Who shall let this world
be beautiful?

Only you
on this hot
and weary morning.

You, child,
on this blistering day.

Who shall let this world
find breath?

Only you, child.
Only you.

Be Kind

Give yourself time.
The world will allow it.

The world will slow its pace

as you breathe deeply
as you gaze
through your kitchen window

at nothing.

Give yourself time

as your children grow tall
as the stars explode.

Give yourself abundance
in the moments
you have taken.

Give yourself time
to examine
the finest small things
and memory.

Breathe.

The world will be here.
It will wait.

Like Flipping a Switch

There was a singular act,
a moment, particular in time,
though no one can say for certain
what it was
or when.

There was the first fingertip
under the page
to begin the chain.

Was it the conception of a single child?
The first utterance of a philosophy or religion?
The acceptance of one economic system
over another?

Perhaps it was a bee
that failed to attend
a necessary flower.

Maybe it was a radiation blast
from a distant star
or God forgetting to bathe properly.

Maybe it was a single book
that did not get written
or a thousand others that did.

We may rightfully blame the tyrants
that have ravaged us
but cannot deny the power
we gave them.

America was always
a rigged game
and all the lies of history
can't change that.

But when was the last moment
when it all could have worked,
when the world might have
dodged this putrid end?

When did grace still have a chance?
It is cowardly to say it never did.

There was a final moment
when we were still
what we hoped ourselves to be.

There must have been.

Try to find it.
Work your way back.

Maybe you will be
the one to understand
the reason
for this knife in our gut

as you take upon yourself
the agony of knowing

of fixing your dead gaze
upon the coming
of all the world's regret.

Here's the Thing

No one knows your name
and still you do it.
No one cares
or even wants you to do this
but you do not stop.
It is embarrassing for them
to see you this way
walking lonely nighttime streets
to admire the darkness
and ask ancient questions
of yourself.
It bothers them
that you read strange books
and write in secret journals.
No one has any use for it
and still you continue.
No one knows your name
except those who pity you
and most likely
no one ever will.
You won't make a dime.
Maybe someday
someone you do not know
will read words
you plucked from nowhere
and decide to keep going
a while longer.
But that's a long shot
so take your comfort now.
No one knows your name
but yours is the unrepentant rapture
of creation.
It is your blood
and you will not stop.

Look in the Mirror

You are an artist.
Are you brave enough
to say so?

Do you have the courage
to own it?

Burning or not,
you are a torch
necessary
and perhaps sufficient.

Please listen:

Boldness
is the swaddling cloth
of glory.

Wear it like armor
and go forth to battle.

There is no other way.

Scream or Fly

Keep a notebook
and pay attention
to the conversations
of young children and animals
when they believe themselves alone.

Take counsel
from the secret dreams
of the supposedly insane.

Cultivate rare flowers for their own sake
and scatter blossoms
among the needy.

Wander forgotten roads
and carve new paths
through unsettled places.

Find ways to fly.

It is easier than you think
and often necessary.

Scream when screaming is required
but do not ignore
your need for silence.

Keep a sharp pencil within reach.

You never know
when you will need it
to create or kill.

You are to the world
as wind is to wildfire.

Live your days
as a riddle
that can never be
undone.

Where Things Are Poppin' the Philadelphia Way

First of all the paper's too thin
and you could stand to eat something, too

but when you climbed into the hula hoop
that was something

it was special I mean

but this paper isn't going to do the job

my words are too heavy
and will rip this stuff to shreds

but go ahead and shake those hips

get your wiggle on
just like the backyard dance parties
we pretended when we were little

you be the teenybopper
and I'll be Dick Clark
feeling you up in the supply closet

I'll write it down but the words
are going to fall
right through this cheap paper

maybe I'll write it on your body
the way Dick might have done it
handing out autographs like indulgences

because rock and roll heaven is real, baby

and it's all flesh and truth
when it comes right down to it

brass tits and blue balls

and the paper I have found
will never contain you
never keep that heaving bosom locked up

because the sweat will dissolve us all
and the paper is so thin

but baby you've got a fine beat
and are so easy to dance to

Weird

Since I exist
I remain

a viable
possibility.

If I did not
exist

I doubt
I could

even convince
myself

that I
am here.

A Stumper

I sometimes wonder
how they do kung fu on Mars.
Yeah, right. Like you don't.

Senescence

We have lost
our soft hearts
and hard reason.

All good things
are gutted
while we laugh
and blame
every victim.

Our history is now
re-written each day
with poor spelling
and bad grammar.

We hardly notice
the killing lies

because it is
so pleasant
to hate what we
do not understand

and understanding
has become a burden
too great to bear.

This was the plan
of course

always the plan.

It has been expected
for many years.

Everything in this world
grows older and finally
loses its way.

We are no different.

Our hard hearts starve
our decrepit brains.

Almost no one
is left to care for us
and we would
hate them for it anyway.

The ugly finish
is our shattered reward
and its moment is at hand.

Praise Jesus Real Loud. I Dare You.

One is tempted to use words
such as "vile," or "grotesque."

"Wicked," perhaps.

"Evil" seems like it should convey
something of substance,
but it never does.

Maybe the best word is "Christian,"
because they do scream the loudest
and usually get their way.

There are other words, like:
"dupe," "dullard," "pawn,"
"simpleton," "idiot," "fool."

"Zealot" is a good one,
though it must be unpacked
and I don't have the strength
just now.

No one understands
what "fascist" even means,
though I am certain it applies.

But what's a coat hanger
among friends, right?

What's a little hemorrhage?

Who even needs health care
or food or shelter?

Education? What even is that?

One is tempted to use words like "karma,"
because it is surely a bitch.
One is tempted to say "vengeance."

Tosh.

Language is a funny game.

It's how we keep score
and this fight
will yet be soaked in blood
and it is far from over.

One Foot Ahead of the Other

We are bound for glory
all of us.

But we go missing
in dead ends
we should have
seen coming

long lonesome stretches
heavy with doubt
and potholes

hairpin curves

hitchhikers with
bad intentions

and side trips
we think make sense
but only bleed us
of our chances.

We lose ourselves
in the comforting dark
and the easy lie of tomorrow.

A few make it all the way

like those who inspired us at the start
but they, too, often faltered.

You still have a chance.

Glory is out there, just down the road.
Go find it if you can.

Here's to You

Here's to the mad
the unloved
the dirty
and the decrepit.

Here's to disappointment
and the loneliness so deep
you can feel it
in your lungs.

And here's to art
and the stars
we wish on

and all the hard paths and desire.

Here's to the dreamers in distress
and the scars that will not fade

the scars we show with pride
when we think to do it

and those we admit we love
when we are able.

Road Trip

Some go missing along the road
choosing dark exits
or strange attractions
of dubious merit.

Empty tanks
and simple exhaustion
take many.

Hitchhikers are common
and sometimes change everything
for good or ill

and often
it is simple hunger
that brings everything to a stop

or fear that the road
is improperly marked
or heading in the wrong direction
or the maps have lied.

Some forge on
through hard miles
and often against the wind
straight into the blinding sun

windows down
singing the old songs
loud and sure
not even worrying
about staying on key.

There are many such roads
and you are on one now.

Someday you will know
if you navigated well
as you arrive at a destination
you only thought you could imagine

perhaps amazed
with all illusion gone

and every road
converging into one
ending as if by broken miracle
in the very same spot
though separated by time
chance
and fickle grace.

To the Great and Glorious Among Us

Read your Dante
and your Shelley.

Memorize whole stanzas
of approved verse
or even long poems
to recite
whenever someone
might be around
to listen.

Dress erratically.

Drink only imported tea
unless a decent red wine
is available.

Wear your hair
as though you live
inside a hurricane.

Eat dainty biscuits
and pine for praise
from the worthies.

Love only women
who are out of reach.

Read your Wordsworth
and your Byron.

Memorize an obscure
passage from Lamb
and mutter it
while sitting on the toilet.

Tell people that nature
is your church.

Bathe once a week
but don't overdo it
with the soap.

Read your Proust
and your Joyce.

Look down your nose
at the commonplace.

Tell yourself that this is how it's done.
Say to new acquaintances that you are a poet.

Believe in your heart
that the ancient gods
are your patrons.

Die someday
and have one or two people
wonder for an hour
what became of you.

Decompose in silence.

This is the destiny
of your breed.

This is the glory
which awaits you

your Valhalla

the best forever
you, Great Titan,
can ever hope to find.

It's All Magic

These are the ancient ways
incantation and blood

pages older than paper

wild women
dancing in the woods

spells and thunder
echoing in caves
ordinary men
would never try

arcane doorways
to another place
hidden
in a wine cask
and deciphered
by starlight.

These are the ways
of rapture
and deadly to tyrants
and preachers

the ancient ways
guiding us
to this moment

you and I
ecstatic and bleeding

and all the world alive

searching the woods
for wild women

naked in our souls

anointed
panting

and ripe
for the dance.

Soirée

I'm with Yeats in the corner
conjuring demons
and over there by the punch bowl
that's Sylvia
happy now if you can believe it
and Ernie's at the bar
with his stories.

And everyone is raging
and just the right
amount of bored
and just the right
amount of drunk.

And I'm in the kitchen
with Allen going mad
and everyone is listening to Neal
tell the damnedest stories.

And I'm in the alley
with good old cummings
naming all the capitals
and Williams is talking medicine
and throwing
hard nouns
all over the place.

And I'm in bed with Dorothy
and her sharp tongue
with Maugham muttering
something profound in the hallway
and Scott escorting Zelda to the patio
for a starlight dance.

And I'm in on the secret with Jack
and I'm in the woods with Flannery
and I'm going to talk with Erskine
if I can get him away
from the typewriter
and find the time.

And all of us are here
all the gang
waiting for you
to kick the door wide
and make it a party.

But hurry, because Yeats knows his stuff
and I'm here to tell you
the demons will eat you right up
if you come at the wrong time
and he's set on finding a love spell
that will do the trick with him and Maud.

Don't even be careful
just come on down.

We're all burning
and there's a seat by the fire
saved just for you.

We've never met but I miss you terribly
everyone does
and we cannot wait
for your wild beauty
to shame us all into love and poems
breathless desire
and fits of wonder.

Good Night

In my dream
you are in
the red chamber
damp with sweat
and whispering.

In my dark dream
you tell stories
no one would ever
willingly hear.

You tell these stories
only to me
and under your breath
and the stench is awful.

In my dream
you are still beautiful
as strange
as that sounds.

It makes me
look forward
to silent death
and the days

when you
will be my equal
even in your beauty

caught in the
red chamber

burnt

and thankfully
all the stories told.

The Loop

Back and forth
from the red room
into the open hallway
through the
pounding door
into the red room
wide awake
sometimes windows
suffice
with their bright flashes
and yards of fabric
back and forth
from the red room
confessing everything
in your loudest voice
detestable gushing
and bound
in living gauze

Raw Nerves and Strangers

quiet in hidden rooms
everyone too numb to panic

telephones which ring forever
dreams of fire and empty houses

memories of laughter
that lonely smell of decay

Final Notice

We will now perform violence
in the common manner.

This is standard as everyone knows
in both process and method.

The common violence
we will perform upon you
is for the good of the people.

The meek who cannot suffer violence
will now be a little happier

and your service is appreciated
as we perform the stealthy violence
in a public place.

We would have you scream
if you can muster the volume.

We would have you show
our mutual scars.

Come with me
from your dark rooms
and let us begin.

I am ready to show no mercy

to take the implements
from their cases
and apply them
to your body.

Relish your fear if you are able.

A final kiss is the last obstacle
and we begin.

Dear Reader

You are out there
somewhere.

I wonder what you are doing
right now
this second

as I sit upon this couch
beside the dog
and listen to my children
bang around upstairs.

You are out there in the night
perhaps reading a book
or watching television.

Maybe you are drinking a beer
or making love.

Maybe you are fighting
with your husband
or wife.

Maybe you are
contemplating murder
or perhaps
suicide

out there somewhere
in this world.

You who are
finally reading
these words

who sit with me
on this couch.

I wonder what you look like
and what your name might be.

I would reach for you
if I were able

but just this moment
we are one

and each of us a ghost.

Thank you for the visit.
You have no idea
what it means to me.

Grateful acknowledgement is made to the following, in which some of these poems previously appeared or have been accepted for publication, sometimes in a slightly different form:

Alien Buddha Press; Alien Buddha Wears a Black Bandana; Alien Buddha Zine; Beatnik Cowboy; Chiron Review; A Compendium of Literary Minds; Fearless; Fever Dreams; GAS: Poetry Art and Music; Horror Sleaze Trash; HSTQ; Litterateur Redefining World; Live Nude Poems; Poetry Feast; Pressure Press Presents; Punk Noir Magazine; The Raw Art Review; Red Fez; Rogue Wolf Press; Rust Belt Press; Rust Belt Review; Rye Whiskey Review; Sacred Chickens; Spillwords; Unlikely Stories Mark V; Winedrunk Sidewalk; Wingnut Brigade; Quail Press.

www.ingramcontent.com/pod-product-compliance
Lightning Source LLC
Chambersburg PA
CBHW030152100526
44592CB00009B/246